For jack and Anna
—M. M.

For Nigel and Annie
—A. A.

PEARSON Glenview, Illinois • Boston, Massachusetts • Chandler, Arizona • Upper Saddle River, New Jersey

This version of Dig Dig Digging published by Pearson.

ISBN 13: 978-0-328-47236-9
ISBN 10:   0-328-47236-0

18   18

Dig Dig Digging

written by
Margaret Mayo

illustrated by
Alex Ayliffe

Diggers

Diggers are good at dig, dig, digging,
scooping up the earth, and lifting and tipping.
They make huge holes with their dig, dig, digging.
They can work all day.

4

Fire Engines

Fire engines are good at race, race, racing.
Look out! Look out! Bright lights flashing.
Hoses at the ready for swoosh, swoosh, swooshing.
They can work all day.

7

Tractors

Tractors are good at pull, pull, pulling,
plowing up the field with a squelch, squelch, squelching.

Round go the wheels. See the dirt flying!
They can work all day. 9

Garbage Trucks

Garbage trucks are good at gobble, gobble, gobbling,
crunching messy garbage bags, squeezing and squashing.
Busy, busy garbage eaters, always gobbling.
They can work all day.

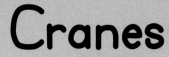

Cranes

Cranes are good at
lift,
lift,
lifting.
Up go the bricks
to the
top of
the building.

12

Down come the pipes,
very
slowly
spinning.
They
can
work
all day.

13

Transporters

Transporters are good at car transporting.
Ramps down, ramps up, shiny cars loading.

All aboard! Off they go—

vroom-vroom-vrooming.

They can work all day.

Dump Trucks

Dump trucks are good at dump, dump, dumping,
carrying heavy loads, and tip, tip, tipping.
Out fall the rocks—

CRASH!

—rumbling and tumbling.

They can work all day.

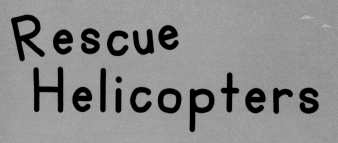

Rescue Helicopters

Helicopters are good at whir, whir, whirring,
hovering and zooming, rotar blades whizzing.
Down comes the rope. Look! Someone needs rescuing!
They can work all day.

18

RoadRollers

Rollers are good at roll, roll, rolling,
pressing hot, sticky tar, smoothing and spreading,
flattening the new road and slowly rolling.
They can work all day.

21

Bulldozers

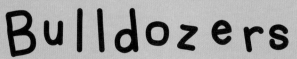

Bulldozers are good at push, push, pushing,
over rough, bumpy ground, scraping and shoving.

Caterpillar treads are grip, grip, gripping.
They can work all day.

Trucks

Trucks are good at l o n g - d i s t a n c e traveling.
Long ones, tall ones, different loads carrying.
Blowing their horns—beep-beep!—their big wheels turning.
They can work all day.

What a busy day! Now it's time for resting.
Brakes on, engines off, the sun is setting.
No beep-beeping, no vroom-vrooming.
Shhh!
They can rest all night.

26